Aretha Tsanga is a student at Adcote School for Girls in Shropshire. Aretha has made 10 publications, 7 poems and 3 short stories and her work appears in different anthologies. She has written some moving poignant pieces. Her passion for poetry writing was ignited in school a few years ago through creative writing club. Aretha wrote all her poems during lockdown. As a young person, she found lockdown very challenging, but her love for writing kept her going. When not writing, typing or thinking about poems, Aretha loves going for walks with her mum, skipping and going on the monkey bars. She also enjoys spending time kicking football in the garden with her young brother, Ainsley.

My mum, my rock, mentor and inspiration. Thank you for believing in me and for supporting me in every way mum. My wonderful sister, Ashley, and my fantastic brother, Ainsley. I love you all.

Aretha Tsanga

THE BLUE CANVAS

AUSTIN MACAULEY PUBLISHERS™

LONDON • CAMBRIDGE • NEW YORK • SHARJAH

A CIP catalogue record for this title is available from the British Library.

ISBN 9781035802791 (Paperback)
ISBN 9781035802807 (ePub e-book)

www.austinmacauley.com

First Published 2023
Austin Macauley Publishers Ltd®
1 Canada Square
Canary Wharf
London
E14 5AA

I have some wonderful people from Adcote School for Girls to thank.

Aretha's Poems

1. I Can't Think of a Poem

I can't think of a poem
And now I am nearly going,
Hang on mum,
Just another one
I could write about
A bear, a pear, even nasal hair

A book, a pirate hook, or even a funny look
Even a spire, a fire, or even a town crier
Would you please be quiet?
You are sounding like a riot.
I can't think of a poem,
And now I am really going.

2. Winter

The coldest season of them all
I wrap myself in a shawl.
As I want to play outside,
My joy of wearing summer clothes denied.
But it's beautiful outside

I realise there is snow
My dad says no
I am not going out today
It's way too cold to play

It's the end of the day
No time to play
No it's tea time
As I hear grandfather's clock chime

We sit by the fire
Whilst we conspire
With hot cocoa in our hands
Listening to my brother's demands

3. Summer

The hottest season of them all
No more spring, winter or fall
I watch the flowers as they grow
It is soothing though very slow

I wake up in the morning from my bed
The blinding sun hits my head
The grass is emerald green
The sun's rays brightly gleam

The smell of flowers fills the air
I can't wait till the summer fair
Swimming at the local pool
Helps us keep cool
What a fantastic day of fun
In the shining sun
What a way to end the day
That was full of play

What a great day I had
With my mum and dad
It was really great

Oh no, it is half past eight
Let the movie marathon commence

4. Autumn

The leaves fall off the trees
I feel the gentle breeze
The sun is away
Yet the birds still play

I see the silver sky
As the birds fly by
My friends and I still play
Until the end of the day

The end of the day will come
Soon we shall end the fun
We play about
Till we hear our mothers shout

We settle down by the fire
That rises higher and higher
My day has come to an end
A day like this shall come again.

5. The Bookshelf

There I stand
Still as calm as I can
Filled with books and magazines
Often enjoying the screen in front of me
I often hear the creatures call it a TV
They stare and watch the pictures
Not even taking a book or magazine
If they aren't going to touch any of my books
Why I am here?
Then one day a creature came to me
And took a book from my shelf
Read the book eagerly
And put it back with care
From then on, it came everyday
To take a book and read it with care

6. There Is a Lady in My Living Room

There is a lady in my living room
I wish she would go away
She is helping my brother get his toys to play
There is a lady in my room
Would she please go away?
I wanted a peaceful day
There is a lady in my living room
She won't go away
I am sitting on the sofa
I have no idea what to say
There is a lady in my living room
She is finally going away
She gives me a hug
And pinches my cheeks
Then mum says,
Wasn't that a lovely day with your auntie
That's the lady who wouldn't go away

7. Dear Fellow Rodent Adventurers

Dear fellow rodent adventurers
I have some advice for you
When climbing up a big steep hill
Don't forget to pop to the loo

Dear fellow rodent adventurers
I have some advice for you
When treading through a panda's bamboo
Don't forget your mother's choux

Dear fellow rodent adventurers
I have some advice for you
When passing through Nepal
Don't forget Kathmandu

Dear rodent adventurers
This is a last piece of advice for you
When going on an adventure
Leave behind all the hullabaloo

8. Hammy Appears

Hammy appeared out of nowhere
And there was no one to show
Where hammy had appeared
Hammy was in a green bag
He was so heavy, the bag begun to sag
Hammy appeared from thin air
Upon my kitchen table
He didn't even come with a label
My mother begun to wrap him in cream and lotions
She begun to mix it all up
Looked like she was making a portion
When hammy was all dressed
She put him in the cabinet
And turned a little knob.
When I came back in the kitchen
I was surprised to see him back on the table
He was hot and crispier than ever
My father brought out a knife
And said "Can't wait to cut in these dears"
Then hammy was cut and a slice put in my plate.

9. The Blessing

Every day is a blessing
The blessing is everyday
The days we are alive
We are happy and we do play
The days we are with family
The times we are with friends
We love those days
We love these days
The days we are with you
We love the days we have alive
The days, the times we have to thrive
If we are all alone
We remember we aren't all alone
For you are there
You are everywhere

10. I'm Stuck

I think am actually stuck
Great, that's just my luck
I'm stuck in the gap
I'm not equipped with a map
I'm stuck in such a flip
Cause I'm stuck
Help me I'm stuck
In the gap between the door
Help me I'm stuck
Just my luck

11. Christmas

It happens once a year
A season full of cheer
We put a tree in the living room
And decorate it with glee
The flock of presents around it we see
We may get snow this time of the year
The amount maybe
Severe or just a smear
Supermarkets flock with shoppers
Trying to find some meat
And staff try to go on their holiday retreat
Christmas, what a great time of the year
For family fun for everyone
Where strife will disappear

12. New Year

New year
New month
New week
New day
New fresh start
New school year
New age
New decade
New millennium
New you
New me,
Happy New Year!

13. The Beach

The waves grey and murky
The sand between my toes
The blinding sun glows
The chatter of people
The sandcastle in construction
The balls bouncing around
The flock of umbrellas
The seagulls nearby
The ice cream truck's jingle
The smell of chips in the fire
The beach, I love to go.

14. What Does Kindness Look Like?

It is a rainbow in the sky
It is a friendly smile
It is helping someone across the street
It is helping cook dinner
It is blue
It is green
It is soft and fluffy
It smells like candy floss
It feels like a blue cloud
It tastes like orange drops
It is patient
It is quiet
It is kind

15. Food

In a big world
With lots of food
There different types
And lots to do
England is famous
For the full English
Italy love its pasta
Asia has wonderful spices
African food can pack a punch
That's what you can have for lunch
Oh! What can we do without you food

16. Friends

Friends come and go
Some old some new
They come in different shapes and sizes
But they are always there for you
Some will fade away
And soon appear
Then, do we trust them or not
Friends, are the best
They help through the life's journey
We cry and laugh together
What are we without friends?

17. I'm sick

My throat is scratchy
I'm struggling to breathe
I'm wrapped up really tight
Tissues spread around me
My nose continuously drips
My body light and fragile
I can almost see my veins
I'm binge-watching films
Lifeless and still
I think my diagnosis
Is that I'm absolutely sick
Oh I'm sick

18. Beauty

What is beauty?
Is beauty a gift
Who is it from
Is beauty six layers of make up
Why do we do it
Is beauty the tightest corset
Why is it there
Is beauty change
Is there a change in beauty

19. I like

I like sun
I like food
I like rain
I like dew
I like fun
I like
I like wind
I like mint
I like me
I like you
I like the weather

20. Change

Should I be scared of it
Is it hiding under my bed
Is it yellow
Is it furry
Does it have sharp claws
And the toughest teeth
Does it haunt me in my dreams
Does it have tough horns
With gargantuan feet
Is change a monster
And will it eat me in the night
Change, change, what are you

21. Bored

I'm bored
If I ask my dad
He'll say wash the dishes
If I ask Mum
She'll say help me cook
If I ask my sister
She'll say go away
If I ask my brother
He'll say play with me
If I ask my grandma
She'll talk about the good-old days
If I ask my grandpa
He'll say go outside
I'm bored
I'm really bored

22. I know

I know what is a flower
I know I've seen the moon
I know I have been through bower
I know what it's like to swoon

I know about the sky
I know what is an ice rink
I know what is in an eye
I know not to drink ink

I know what is a book
I know what is a pen
I know what is brook
I know a girl called Adrienne
I know everything

23. Running

I'm running
With no place to go
No destination
Or a place to call home

I'm running
With the wind in my hair
A pain in my ankle
And no one to care

I'm running
The sky is darkening now
And the road is now ending
Sweat drips from my brow

24. Dear Human

Dear Human
Would you stop walking through me
I was a human too, you know
And stop leaving your plates everywhere
It doesn't hurt to vacuum in a while
Would you pick up your clothes
Your diet is made of junk food
Actually, it would probably be best
If you moved out
Yours sincerely
Ghost

25. Why

Why are you here
Why aren't you there
I thought we were friends
Why are you so unaware
Of the fact you hurt
Why now?

26. Goodbye

A word we often use
A word with a sad meaning
A word that can be hard to say
A word that can lead to tears
A word of great status
A word……
I dread to say
Goodbye

27. Dear Mum

Most confident
Only one I see
Trustworthy
Happy
Extraordinary
Resilient

Wonderful
Important
Fabulous
Engaged in everything you do

Never ending love
Understandable
Rude, never
Super good fashion-sense
Extremely fun to be with

Thank you for all you do
For me and everyone else
We don't know how to repay you
Love you infinity
And beyond

28. The Orchid

Your unique beauty
Your special way of blooming
Your everlasting glow

29. Fear

I can feel it building in up inside
My stomach begins to clench
I feel sweat trickling down my forehead
I fear I might pass out

30. The World

You will always spin
You continue to provide
Even more than our sin